CONJUNCTIONS SAY

"JOIN US!"

by Michael Dahl

illustrated by Maira Chiodi

PICTURE WINDOW BOOKS
a capstone imprint

2

Conjunctions are words that join other words or groups of words called phrases and clauses.

Conjunctions can make long, long sentences.

MY FRIENDS AND MY DOG

AND I WENT CAMPING

BECAUSE we like being outdoors,

BUT WE WERE NOT SURE IF THE SKY WOULD BE CLOUDY OR SUNNY.

Coordinating conjunctions are the words "for," "and," "nor," "but," "or," "yet," and "so." They join words or groups of words that are equally important.

Here's your first test, scouts, **so** do your best, **for** you are being graded. Join these words! Go!

You **and** me!

DELICIOUS RIGHT LOUD ME YOU MESSY LEFT BEAUTIFUL

9

Coordinating conjunctions can turn two sentences into one.

First we joined single words, **and** now we'll join sentences!

SO OR

They don't have much, YET

Theo wants chocolate cake,

I love my dog, BUT her

they always share.

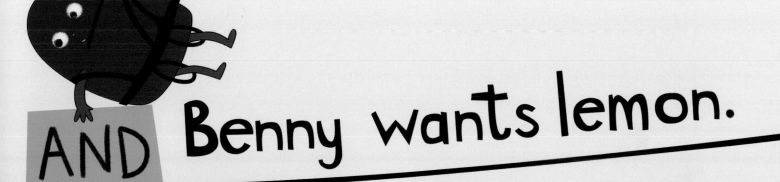

AND Benny wants lemon.

snoring keeps me awake.

Her snoring keeps me awake.

15

Conjunctions can give you a choice.

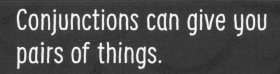

Conjunctions can give you pairs of things.

Awesome scary story! I'm so glad the brave brother **and** sister destroyed the monsters!

I wanted a funny story before bed.

Me toooooo!

Yeah, like Luke **and** Leia!

The monsters were just like Dracula **and** Frankenstein!

So spooky **and** goosebumpy!

Some conjunctions always work together in pairs. They're called correlative conjunctions. Common ones are "either/or," "neither/nor," "if/then," and "not only/but also."

If it doesn't rain in the morning, then I'm going bird-watching.

If it *does* rain in the morning, then I'm staying in bed!

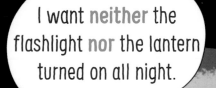

Conjunctions can help explain when, why, and how things happened.

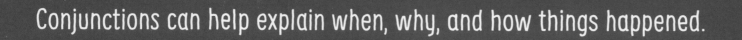

I have so many ideas jumbled up in my head. All the things that happened today. So much! Maybe I should write them down. How will it all make sense?

AFTER we ate our hot dogs, THEN we made s'mores. NEXT we sang our scout song, AND THEN we listened to a scary story BECAUSE we all voted for one.. SINCE it got really cold, AND the fire was going out, we all went in our tents AND got ready for bed, BUT I couldn't sleep. I think it was the hot dogs. Is 12 too many? SO I turned on my light AFTER I got under the covers AND decided to write this all down BEFORE I forget. ONCE I finish writing, I hope I fall fast asleep.

While many conjunctions are small and plain, some are big and fancy.

if

IN THE EVENT THAT

but

EXCEPT

although

NOTWITHSTANDING

23

Big or small, conjunctions always bring things together.

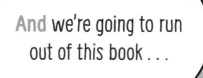

CONJUNCTION JAMBOREE

Conjunctions are words that join other words. Common conjunctions include "and," "but," "or," "if," "because," and "then."

Conjunctions connect words that give you a choice between two things.

Do you want peanut butter OR jelly?

Would you like a leopard OR a blobfish as a pet?

Conjunctions can combine things.

I want a leopard AND a blobfish!

Conjunctions can tell you when or why things happen.

I'm going to the zoo, AND THEN I will stop by the aquarium.

I hate thunderstorms BECAUSE of all the lightning!

Conjunctions can help make one long sentence by joining two or more sentences.

I couldn't finish reading the scary book.

I returned the book to the library.

I checked out another book that wasn't scary at all.

I couldn't finish reading the scary book, SO I returned it to the library,

AND I checked out another book that wasn't scary at all.

ABOUT THE AUTHOR

Michael Dahl is the author of more than 200 books for children and has won the AEP Distinguished Achievement Award three times for his nonfiction. He is the author of the bestselling *Bedtime for Batman* and *You're a Star, Wonder Woman!* picture books. He has written dozens of books of jokes, riddles, and puns. He likes to play with words. In grade school, he read the dictionary for fun. Really. Michael is proud to say that he has always been a noun. A PROPER noun, at that.

ABOUT THE ILLUSTRATOR

Maira Chiodi's colorful, joyful work has appeared in magazines, books, games, and a variety of other products. As a child in Brazil, Maira spent hours cutting paper, painting, and reading—creating wildly imaginative worlds all her own. Today she feels lucky to be able to create and share her illustrations and designs with kids and grown-ups around the world. She divides her time between Canada and Brazil, finding inspiration for her art in nature, animation, and the culture of her native country.

GLOSSARY

clause—a group of words that includes a subject and a predicate (a word or group of words that tells what the subject does or what is done to the subject)

conjunction—a word that joins other words or groups of words

coordinating conjunction—a kind of conjunction that joins sentences or parts of sentences that are equal

correlative conjunction—a kind of conjunction that always works in pairs, such as "either/or"

phrase—a group of words that expresses a thought but is not a complete sentence

subordinating conjunction—a kind of conjunction that ties an incomplete thought to a complete thought

THINK ABOUT IT

1. Which conjunction would you use to give someone a choice between two flavors of ice cream? Use it in the form of a question.

2. The following sentences contain correlative conjunctions. How would you fill in the blanks? IF I pass my test, THEN _____.
NOT ONLY is my dog _____, BUT she is ALSO _____.

READ MORE

Cleary, Brian P. *But and For, Yet and Nor: What Is a Conjunction?* Words Are CATegorical. Minneapolis: Millbrook Press, 2010.

Fandel, Jennifer. *What Is a Conjunction?* Parts of Speech. North Mankato, MN: Capstone Press, 2013.

Walton, Rick. *Just Me and 6,000 Rats: An Adventure in Conjunctions.* Layton, UT: Gibbs Smith, 2011.

INTERNET SITES

Enchanted Learning: Grammar: Conjunction
https://www.enchantedlearning.com/grammar/partsofspeech/conjunctions

Grammaropolis: The Conjunctions
https://www.grammaropolis.com/conjunction.php

Schoolhouse Rock: Conjunctions
https://www.youtube.com/watch?v=RPoBE-E8VOc

LOOK FOR ALL THE PARTS OF SPEECH TITLES

INDEX

Editor: Jill Kalz
Designer: Lori Bye
Production Specialist: Katy LaVigne
The illustrations in this book were created digitally.

Picture Window Books are published by Capstone
1710 Roe Crest Drive, North Mankato, Minnesota 56003
www.capstonepub.com

Library of Congress Cataloging-in-Publication Data
Names: Dahl, Michael, author.
Title: Conjunctions say "join us!" / by Michael Dahl.
Description: 1st ed. | North Mankato, Minnesota : Picture Window Books, [2020] |
Series: Nonfiction picture books. Word adventures : parts of speech
Identifiers: LCCN 2019004139| ISBN 9781515840992 (library binding) | ISBN 9781515841074 (paperback) | ISBN 9781515841036 (eBook PDF)
Subjects: LCSH: English language—Conjunctions—Juvenile literature. | English language—Grammar—Juvenile literature.
Classification: LCC PE1345 .D34 2020 | DDC 428.2—dc23
LC record available at https://lccn.loc.gov/2019004139

All internet sites appearing in back matter were available and accurate when this book was sent to press.

Printed and bound in China.
001654